AF405622

THE
HIDDEN
PLACE

STUDY GUIDE

GOING DEEPER

CONNIE VICTORIA VOLK

COPYRIGHT

Copyright © 2023 Connie Victoria Volk

All rights reserved. No part of this book may be reproduced by any means, graphic, electronic, or mechanical, including photocopying, recording, taping or by any information storage retrieval system without written permission of the author except in the case of brief quotations embodied in critical articles and reviews.

Cover design by Solutions Website Design.
Adapted from a painting by the author.

ISBN: 9798986495637

PREFACE

A stirring began in my heart a few months after publishing *The Hidden Place*. A stirring for something more, something deeper.

The story of the hidden place had risen from the pages of the book. It stood there for all to see. But the Lord prompted me to dig deeper into scripture, to reveal the underlying structure. I wanted to see the master blueprint. I wanted to lay bare the Rock on which the footings were poured.

If the foundation was solid, so would be the girders that rose toward the sky.

So I knew my work was not finished. Closer inspections would need to be made. Again, led by the still small voice (I Kings 19:12), I ventured below the surface of the hidden place. I eagerly undertook this task, both for myself and for those who were hungry for yet more of the sweet honey of the Word.

I now share this continuing journey. As we explore together the underlying foundational truths, we will come to recognize the grand design of both this book and our very lives.

Get ready for a taste of more!

INTRODUCTION

This study guide is divided into four practical growth sections.

Prophetic Declarations:
At the end of nearly every chapter, you will find a declarative sentence or two about how God wants to bless you. That blessing is for everyone.

How is it received?
1. Agree with God about the declaration.
2. Declare it *aloud* (Job 22:21 AMPC) throughout the day and before retiring at night.
3. Write it on the "Declarations" page at the end of the book.
4. Be aware of how these declarations are gradually changing your attitudes to reflect those of the Creator.

Matters of the Heart:
You will find designated "Matters of the Heart" to ponder. They are interspersed throughout the chapters. You can choose to either gloss over them, come back to them at a more opportune time or open your heart's door to light up what has been kept hidden within. The more you bring before Him, the more healing your heart will experience. May this bring a growing intimacy with the King.

Writing His Word on your Heart:
"Thy Word have I hid in my heart that I might not sin against You (Ps. 119:11).

Before I ever felt led to begin writing *The Hidden Place*, the scripture passages of Col. 3:2-4 and Eph. 3:14-20 called out to me.

4

For two to three months I meditated on them, committed them to memory and then waited for God to reveal the hidden nuggets within. I sensed I was only skimming the surface and not absorbing the spiritual nutrients in those scriptures. The reality of those truths had yet to become one with me before they could be expressed in words.

For your heart to also experience this type of immersion, I encourage you to memorize these same two core passages. They form the scriptural foundation for the entire devotional.

Always begin writing His Word on your heart by asking for the Holy Spirit's help. Remember to thank Him for all progress. He loves to bless, and Prov. 4:20-23 will cheer you along the way.

The memorization method that works best for me is to read *aloud* ten times the verse or passage I've chosen. Then I copy it to review throughout the day. Right before getting into bed, I again read it *aloud* ten times. This allows my heart to meditate on it as I sleep. After that, I keep reviewing it until I can share it any time or anywhere.

Set a goal for yourself. Choose someone to help keep you accountable. Keep the passages fresh in your focus while you travel through the study guide.

All scripture in this study guide will be coordinated with the book and taken from *The Passion Translation*, Second Edition unless otherwise noted. If you are using a different edition or a phone with the Holy Bible app, developer Life.Church, just be alert to which footnote applies. If no translation is mentioned for an Old Testament scripture, feel free to use the one of your choice.

Transformation:
"And he has taught you to let go of the lifestyle of the ancient man, the old self-life, which was corrupted by sinful desires that spring

from delusions. Now it's time to be made new by every revelation that's been given to you. And to be transformed as you embrace the glorious Christ-within as your new life and live in union with him! For God has re-created you all over again in his perfect righteousness, and you now belong to him in the realm of true holiness" (Eph. 4:22-24).

You will find the theme of transformation in the above scripture passage reiterated time and again as you journey through this study guide. The shifts will occur in four general areas.
1. Receiving the love of God
2. Surrendering your will and trusting His
3. Feeling at ease in the presence of God
4. Resembling more closely the image of your heavenly Father

Feel free to write in this book. Join the adventure. Be encouraged. The more you invest in going deeper, the more you will be blessed.

A WORD FROM THE AUTHOR

An Overview

Read pp. 17-25.

"The Mystery" poem is found at the end of both chapters one and thirty-three. It was the very first one ever given to me by the Holy Spirit. Little did I realize at its writing on April 3, 2014, where the next nine years would lead. This poem serves as bookends for the entire **Hidden Place** devotional. One can spend a lifetime navigating this mystery.

The themes are set in Chapter One. The whole book is a mystery for each one of us personally. We will explore the Lord's way of transforming us throughout our faith ***"Journey"*** (p. 19) on this earth. The best way to navigate the journey is by going ***"Low"*** (p. 17) on this ***"Boat Ride of Life."***

The gifts we have received make us all a part of God's "tapestry" of love to serve one another. In this study, we will begin to understand the mystery of His grace flowing through us and changing us into His likeness (I Peter 4:10 TPT).

Take note, as best you can, of where you are now as you peek through His "open door." Do it again at the conclusion of the book. You will find your progress remarkable.

The more diligent and open your search in the Holy Spirit realm, the greater your treasure will be at the end. Engage your heart and be open to His love. Do not be afraid. Take a chance on God. Invite Him in, and He will radically transform you.

Chapter 1

"The Journey"
(the poem)

1. Review the poem again.
How can you relate to the author's journey?

Looking back on your journey of life, where do you see the past interwoven with the present?

How is it affecting your future, positively or negatively?

What are the Lord's plans for your journey?
Eph. 1:5-6

When did this long-range plan begin?
Eph. 1:9

When will it come to completion?
Eph. 1:10

The Journey
(the chapter)

1. Who is the main character of the book?

2. To the Lord, are you just "Everyone" or "Anyone?"
Ps. 32:8-9

Is. 49:16; Ps. 27:10

Luke 10:20

II Peter 1:3

At a deeper level of meaning (Ps. 92:5b), is there an additional possibility that the main character is the body of Christ being transformed into the Bride of Christ?

3. Would you like to be invited by the Lord into the "hidden place?"

A key to entering is an attitude of humility.
Refer to the poem *"Low"* on pages 17-18.
Who is our perfect model? Phil. 2:6-9

How can we show humility? I Peter 5:5-6

What will be God's response?

Worship Opportunity: The song, "Humble Thyself in the Sight of the Lord" (Maranatha Singers).

4. Have you ever found yourself growing weary or stressed as the newness of your life has lost its excitement? Give some examples.

Have you ever sensed there must be something more?

What is the symbolism of the polished, brown shoes and their change in appearance?

What role might self-effort play in this?

While on the interstate of life, whose hands were on the steering wheel?

What became the incentive for getting off that road?

5. Who is the tall, willowy figure? John 14:16-17 footnote.

Why is His face hidden?

Why does the writer feel no fear? John 16:13-14 Discuss.

Consider how the Holy Spirit smoothed the way (Ps. 5:8b) for the traveler in the following instances…
   the longing in his heart for something more
   the yearning for peace
   the fellow travelers
   the refreshing water
   the renewed energy and hope
   the melody in his heart
   the delivery of the key to unlock the door.
   the door opening at his touch

How has He guided and directed your journey up to this point? List specific examples.

Turn to the Prophetic Declarations pages at the end of the Study Guide. Refer to the instructions in the Introduction if necessary. Copy the first declaration, "I am His guest, and I know I am about to be transformed." See: Song of Sg. 2:13.
How prophetic (forth telling) this declaration is!

"The Mystery"

1. What is the mystery? Col. 1:26-27

Can you sense His excitement as His plans for you unfold? Will you allow yourself to let go and have "fun" …finding out more about who He really is, and who you are? Col.3:3-4

When at the end of your physical life and entering eternity, what part will this mystery play? Col. 3:3-4

How exciting to see the coming chapters reveal more of this mystery! Stay tuned.

Chapter 2

"Who Would Have Thought"

1. Read the poem at the beginning of this chapter.

What did Abraham say about ashes?
Gen. 18:27

What do ashes symbolize?
Esther 4:1
Job 42:6
Matt. 11:21

2. Who can change or rearrange situations in our lives?
Is. 61:1-3
Rom. 8:28

What dynamic is at work in Prov. 13:12 (NIV)?

The Hidden Place

1. Read Ps. 91:1-16, 17:8; 61:4, 94:23b
Where is the hidden place?

Who is the hidden place?

What does He say to us there?

What safety and security do we find there?

The journey of discovering our true identities begins and ends where?

Prophetic Declaration: "Tonight I will sleep in peace." (Again, review the instructions given in the Introduction.)
What declarations about sleep are found in the following scriptures?
Ps.3:5

Ps. 4:8

As His peace surrounds and protects us, we are strengthened. When our hearts are at rest, our entire beings receive His flow of life.
Worship Opportunity: The song "You Are My Hiding Place" by Selah.

"The Source"

1. Who is the Source of Love? Who is the ultimate Pearl of Great Price? Eph. 3:17-19

A Taste of More:
Find a quiet place and time to meditate on and absorb the truth of Eph. 3:17. Do not hesitate to do this time and time again.
Open the eyes of your heart (Eph. 1:18) to see the process described in *The Source* and to experience it for yourself.
It marks the beginning of the path of intimacy in the hidden place.

Begin your journey of Hiding His Word in your Heart with Col. 3:2-4. Review the pattern given in the Introduction to this study guide.

Chapter 3

"The Circle of Life"

Where does God sit?
Is. 40:22

All our planets, moons and sun are in what shape?
Our planets and moons orbit the sun in circles.
Does it seem part of a natural pattern to have our lives described in terms of a circle?

Where are our lives hidden away?
Col. 3:2-4

How is God described?
Deut. 33:27

Micah 5:2

If we are in Him, will our circle of life ever end?

Have we ever had the self-centered idea life revolves around us?
List a few recent examples.

The Sharing

1. What was the prophetic declaration at the end of the last chapter?

What does the author say in the morning?

Did Father's flow of life bring restoration?

What areas are being addressed in the following verses?
Jer. 30:17

Ex. 15:26

Ps. 51:12

What does Jesus tell us to do in John 16:24?

Ask Him for restoration tonight before going to bed and for His abundant grace for the next day.

2. Read Ps. 74:3-7 (footnote for v. 6).
Matters of the Heart:
Are we only physical beings making our way through life?

What is the psalmist asking the Lord to do?

How has the enemy tried to mar the image of God within you?

Why do we sometimes strain against becoming the best God our Father created us to be?

If we are created as unique individuals, is it in our interest to be down on ourselves or compare ourselves to others?

Jesus said we must love others as we love ourselves (Mark 12:31). But shame, guilt or unforgiveness may be a roadblock. As you bring these before the Lord, He will be quick to forgive.

3. Refer to the fourth paragraph of the chapter. Will our journeys ever really end? Where will they continue if we are in Christ?

"Free"

1. What is the truth about the "me" I am free to be?
Jer. 1:5

Ps. 139:13-18 (v. 13 footnote)

I am an original. There is no one like me in the universe. What simple instructions are given in Prov. 12:9a?

Writing God's Word on your Heart:
Keep reviewing Col. 3:2-4 and let it be imprinted on your heart.

Chapter 4

"White As Snow"

1. This poem illustrates the Father's love in action through Whom?
Is. 1:18

2. Where does snow comes from?
Job 37:6; Is. 55:10
Job 38:22

With what is snow associated?
Ps. 51:7

What is the significance of His hair?
Dan. 7:9
Rev. 1:14 (footnote)

Worship Opportunity: Soak in the song "As White as Snow" by Maranatha Singers. Music speaks directly to our hearts and imprints truth there.

The Shepherd

1. What is revealed about the Shepherd and His work?
Ps. 23:1-3a (footnotes)

What does God say about His protective eye and His care?
Ps. 139:7-12

Prov. 15:3

Jer. 23:24
Heb. 4:13

Is the Good Shepherd's presence determined by our feelings or ability to sense Him?

2. What is included in the Greek understanding of the word "heal?"
Mark 10:52 (footnote)

Healing is part of our inheritance. Let's claim it!

3. Review the third paragraph of the chapter.
Give personal examples of love and compassion breaking down barriers.

To whom can you show love this week?

Consider the author's journey to freedom. What worked together to bring that release?

"The Yoke"

1. Read Matt. 11:28-30 with all the footnotes.
What new insights do you find here?

Chapter 5

"Matching"

Transformation:
What do you notice within as you see yourself becoming more at one with Him?

Are there any changes in your emotions? Read I John 4:15-17 (v. 17 footnotes).

(Refer to the Introduction if necessary.)

The Fire of Love

1. Is He capable of holding the world in His hands? Is He limitless? (sixth paragraph of the chapter)
Is, 40:12

Ps. 24:1-2

Job 38

2. We all come to Jesus as cracked leaky vessels.
(Read the third paragraph from the end of the chapter.)
Track the transformation that took place in the Shulamite. She becomes a pattern for us.
Song of Sg. 4:5

Song of Sg. 4:13a

Song of Sg. 7:5

Song of Sg. 8:10

In what mighty way did God use the broken pitchers in the hands of Gideon's men?
Judges 7:15-22

How can He use us to speak into the lives of others?

What can we do right now for someone who needs healing.

3. Notice the Shepherd's daily delight in caring for us.
Is. 40:11

Ps. 23:2-3 (footnotes)

I Peter 2:25

John 6:35 (footnote)

At the end of the chapter, do physical needs become less important in the presence of the Lord?

"Our Love for Him"

1. How does our love affect Him?
Song of Sg. 4:9 (footnote)

Song of Sg. 4:11 (footnote)

Song of Sg. 8:9

Ps. 8:4-5

Ps. 16:3

Prov. 8:31

Zeph. 3:17

2. How has His love changed us?
Song of Sg. 2:8-10

Song of Sg. 1:15

Rom. 8:37 (footnotes)

Writing His Word on your Heart:
Is Col. 3:2-4 becoming a natural part of your heart? The more you
share it with others, the more you become comfortable with it.

Chapter 6

"The Realm Within"

1. The realm within is located between which two places?
II Cor. 4:18

2. What is released in this internal place?
II Cor. 4:6

II Peter 1:19b (footnote)

3. What is one of the results?
Heb. 4:12 (footnote d)

The Seed

1. How long will His seeds in us endure?
I Peter 1: 22-23

2. Who plants good seeds?
Matt. 13:37

3. Who is the ultimate Seed?
I Peter 2:2 (footnote)

4. What does being one with Christ mean for you?
I Cor. 3:16-17

I Cor. 6:17-19 (v. 17 footnote)
5. How does Song of Sg. 5:4-5a parallel the last four paragraphs
of the chapter?

Transformation:
What bad seeds have been planted in your heart?

What crop will those seeds produce?

What needs to be done with them?
Matt. 15:13

6. Read the last paragraph of the chapter.
Life is not a dead end but an ongoing adventure in Him.
How can we cultivate an "air of expectation" about tomorrow? Our
years on earth? Our time in eternity?

"The Word/The Mirror"

1. Who unveils our faces?
II Cor. 3:16 and 17 (footnote)

2. What process do we go through after the unveiling?
II Cor. 3:18 (first three footnotes)

Freedom comes from this metamorphosis! The inferior mindsets of ourselves are left behind as we are transformed into God's original design.

Chapter 7

"Take Heart"

1. What truths allow us to take heart when facing a problem?
Deut. 31:6-8

Matt. 28:20

Is. 41:13

Ps. 98:1

2. What should be our strategy before entering battle?
Ps. 98:1-6

II Chron. 20:20-30?

Matters of the Heart:
What battles are you facing right now?

How could you employ this strategy?

The Stronghold

1. Read the chapter, taking notes on the process the writer went through to be free.

2. In your journey through life, what role have your emotions played in your progress or lack of progress?

3. What traumas from your past have triggered you to overreact in the present?

4. As you search your heart, identify any unforgiveness of self, others or God associated with those overreactions.

5. You can release those to Christ Who forgives, and then let His peace flow through those wounds in your heart.

6. List any lies of the enemy you are believing. Beside them, list the truths. You can reject the lies out loud now and speak God's truths instead.

7. Incidents from the past can fester and become "little foxes" (Song of Sg.2:15 footnote), robbing us of our intimacy with the Lord. Surrender them to Him now and let Him wash them away.

8. Describe the freedom that has come to you.

9. For more insight into these matters, I recommend the book, *deep relief Now* by Dennis and Dr. Jen Clark. For video demonstrations and further teaching go to www.forgive 123.com or to www.kingdomlife church.us.

"Sunshine"

1. What do we learn about sunshine in the natural realm and then in the spiritual realm?
Ps. 74:16

Job 9:7

Joshua 10:12-13

Matt. 5:45

Is. 60:19-20

Mal. 4:2

Is. 30:26

Rev. 21:23

2. What role does light play in the darkness of our inner realm?
II Peter 1:19 (the last 5 footnotes)

Is. 9:1-2

Chapter 8

"The Joy of Love"

1. How is the joy of love expressed in these scriptures?
Ps. 51:12, 15-17

Ps. 45:1, 7-8, 15

Heb. 12:2b (footnote g)

He has done His part. Our part is to receive and celebrate all God is for us. We respond in joy to all God wants to do in us. We are accepted in the Beloved.

The Veranda of Love

1. Note how love and joy are interconnected in this chapter.

2. Can our natural hunger at times be satisfied with nutrients from the heavenly realm?
John 4:5-8 (footnotes)

John 4:31-34 (footnotes)

From where did this food come?
Ex. 16:14-21

How was this foreshadowing of food from heaven fulfilled?
John 6:30-35(footnote f)

3. What heals the wounds of our hearts? See paragraph six.

What healing balm is spoken of here?
Song of Sg. 4:14 (footnote f)

4. What more do we learn about wounds?
Heb. 12:1 (footnote b)

Transformation:
List any wounds in your heart blocking the pathway of love
between you and the Lover of your soul.

"Consummation"

1. Is our concept of time often short-sighted, lacking imagination
or foresight?
Let's practice using the eyes of our hearts to see and imagine what
is talked about in the following verses. Take your time and relish
the experience. Allow it to lead you into worship.
Eph. 1:21-23; 3:21

Point to Ponder:
Will the relationship between the body of Christ and the heavenly
Bridegroom ever be complete or finalized?
Song of Sg. 8:14

The Prophetic Declaration at the end of this chapter is so encouraging. Speaking it aloud leads us into intimacy with the King.

Chapter 9

"My Everything"

1. Who is the originator of changes inside of us?
John 6:44

2. How does His name qualify Him for this title?
Ex. 3:14

3. Read Song of Sg. 2:3a. Try asking the Lord each morning,
"Who or what do You want to be for *me* today?" Keep a journal of
His answers. Focus on Him and His role in your life throughout the
day. Before going to sleep, give Him thanks. At the end of a
month, you will be amazed at how your relationship has grown.

The Library

1. Refer to paragraphs eleven through fourteen. What two
elements refresh, strengthen and nourish our bodies and souls on
our earthly journey?
List the benefits of taking in these elements.
John 6:53-58 (footnotes)

2. For which bread should we be passionate?
John 6:27 (footnote a)

3. Who is the rock?
I Cor. 10:1-4 (footnote j)

What do we learn about drinking of the Lord?

Ps. 36:9

Why was no one feeble?
Ps. 105:37 KJV

Worship Opportunity: The song "New Wine" by Hillsong

"Touch Me"

1. How does touching Him involve our hearts?
Luke 8:8

Luke 8:18

2. Does Jesus know when we reach out to touch Him?
Luke 8:45 (footnote)
What are the benefits of touching Him?

Matters of the Heart:
What can I do every day to make a practice of reaching out to touch Him in faith?

Writing His Word on your Heart:
Have the truths in Col. 3:2-4 become absorbed within you? Do they seem real within you?
How are your ways of thinking being changed?

Continue to review these scriptures from time to time.

Begin permanently writing Eph. 3:14-20 on your heart.

Refer to the Introduction again, if necessary.

33

Chapter 10

"The Path of Life"

1. Read Prov. 3:5-10 as though it were your first time. Notice how often the following words are used: completely, every, all, whatever, wherever, undivided, everything, very best, uncontainable.
What message is being conveyed by these words?

Whose guidance is this?

2. What part does my will and conscience play in staying on the path of life?
Prov. 3:3 (footnote)

Transformation:
1. How am I allowing Him to guide me?

2. In what way is there a mindfulness of Him as I go about my daily tasks?

3. What beginning steps can I take today in that direction?

4. What are the promised rewards?
Prov. 3:1-10

The Blessing

First the Shepherd feeds us with food from the natural realm and then, more importantly, with food from the spiritual realm—His words of life.

1. What do we learn about spiritual feasting from the following scriptures?
Ps. 3:8

Ps. 34:8 (footnote)

Song of Sg. 8:5

2. Who is our banquet?
Ps. 63:5

Ps. 23:5

3. What does Jesus feast upon?
John 4:32 (footnote)

4. What fruits is Jesus forming within us that He can feast upon?
Song of Sg. 4:14 (footnotes)

5. For an overall understanding of this dynamic, read Song of Sg. 4:16-5:1 (footnotes). Rephrase it in your own words.

6. What other blessings are available to us?
Deut. 28:1-14

Prophetic Declaration: What a powerful one to declare each day and any time you are feeling drained.
As you go along, some specific ones may seem to be made especially for you. Declare them aloud often.

"The Boat"

1. What do the following scriptures say about God "seeing the path and knowing the way?"
Is. 43:16

Is. 51:10

Ps. 77:19

Matters of the Heart:
Recount a situation of coming to a Red Sea time in your life when there was no way out and no way through. What was the outcome?

Chapter 11

"The Process"

1. In this process of sanctification, we are being set apart for God's special use and purpose. We have already been made perfect in Christ and are seated in the heavenlies with Him.
How does Eph. 2:6 (footnote) express that?

However, while we are also here on earth, the yearning of our hearts is for what?
Eph. 3:18-19

2. Who is the one in charge of this?
Phil.2:13

The Bible in Basic English states it this way. "For it is God who is the cause of your desires and of your acts, for His good pleasure."

3. What role do we then play in this process?
John 15:4-5

4. Before He could shine His light in us, from what did He have to rescue us?
Col. 1:13

The Process

The chapter itself continues the progressive unveiling of truth to set our hearts free of the enemy lies.
Transformation:

1. Can you identify any lies you may have inadvertently taken in? If so, practice the process described in paragraph ten. Breathe in the breath of the Holy Spirit and breathe out the bad. Continue until you feel His joy and peace rising to the surface.

2. Read paragraph thirteen. Find a Bible verse of your own choosing. With the Holy Spirit's assistance, try this process for yourself.

"The Yearning"

1. How is the yearning in this poem different from that in the first poem of the chapter?

2. How has the author gone deeper in her relationship with the Lord?

Matters of the Heart:
Have you gone deeper in your relationship with Him?

Practice wrapping your arms around a pillow and freely expressing your own personal yearnings to the King. He loves you and will never turn you away.

Writing His Word in your Heart:
If the four paragraphs of Eph. 4:15-20 seem daunting, try dividing them up into smaller sections. You might also place scripture cards around your home to refresh your memory.

Chapter 12

"I Know"

1. Give examples of His hurt and pain?
Is. 52:14

Is. 53:3-5

2. Why was His emptiness so deep?
Matt. 27:46

3. How deeply does He understand what we are going through?
John 11:35

4. In part, what did His pain and suffering make possible for us?
Is. 43:1

Ponder those truths until they move from your head and become implanted in your heart.

The Yielding

1. About what are we cautioned?
Ex. 23:32-33

Matt. 6:21

2. What is the danger of holding tightly to our idols?
Ps. 106:36

3. How can pride and the opinions of others be factors in the formation of our idols?
John 5:44

4. How did The Most High deal with pride in this instance?
Dan.4:28-37

Matters of the Heart:
Is there anything taking precedence over your personal time with Him?

Is there anything clutched tightly in your hands that you are unwilling to let go of?

Review the chapter. What is it within you that must yield before you can walk in freedom?

5. What happens next?
Ps. 3:3-4 (footnote)

6. How do you then stay on the right track?
Ps. 119:9

Worship Opportunity:
The Song "Change My Heart O God" by Vineyard

Prophetic Declaration:

Even if you sense your heart is not yet fully healed or your will fully yielded, in faith declare that it is as you present yourself before God. Job 2:1

Your words have life and power. Prov. 18:21
Watch what God will do.

"Transformation"

1. How are we inwardly transformed by the Holy Spirit?
Rom. 12:1-2

2. How do we change the way we think?
Eph 4: 22-24

A summary of the process:
1. Let go of that old self-life. We've already cut those ties. (Eph. 3:3)

2. Know that you are a new creation. You've already been recreated all over again in His righteousness. You are one with Him. (Col. 3:4)

3. Every time you receive a revelation of who He really is, present yourself before God and proclaim who you really are. (I John 4:17b)

For example: I am Your dearly loved child, and I am dressed in the righteousness of Christ. I am dead to the "old man." I no longer listen to the echo of his voice; I don't think or act like he did. I have Your favor, and I am filled with Your power which constantly energizes me. Thank you, Father, that today I can be patient, loving and kind to the people I meet.

Chapter 13

"One to Behold"

1. Describe the One to Behold.
Dan. 7:9-10

2. Describe His might.
Is. 40:18, 23-26

Ps. 2:5

3. Describe His throne room.
Is. 6:1-4

The Door

1. In this chapter what steps are taken to arrive at peace? There are
at least nine of them. You may want to add others from your
personal experience.

2. Why is there no need to fear our "final journey?"
Ps. 23:4

"Peace"

1. Is peace a person?
Is. 9:6
When we receive Jesus into our hearts, peace is received also. It is
our *awareness* of that peace which must be cultivated to full
fruition.
2. How prevalent is our awareness of peace meant to be?
II Cor. 13:11

Jude 1:2

Ps. 4:8

Is. 26:3

Luke 2:29

Rom. 16:20

Col. 3:15 (footnote)

3. What part does thankfulness play in our awareness of peace?
Col 3:15

Chapter 14

"The Field"

1. What do we learn about preparation before intimacy with the Presence of the Lord?
Prov. 24:27 ESV

Matt. 25:1-13 (footnote c)

James 4:8-10

The Fields of Grace

1. What are some of the end results of going with the King when He calls?
I Cor. 6:17 (footnote)

II Cor. 3:11

2. What happens after we have tasted the goodness of the Lord?
Ps. 119:80-82

3. Is the restoration at the end of the chapter only on a physical level?
Mark 10:52 (footnote)

Matters of the Heart:
Think back to a time when joy filled your entire being.

From what did joy set you free?

Is there anything holding you back now from giving yourself permission to let go, enjoy life and be filled with joy?

Can we choose joy anyway?

"Joy"

1. What do we learn from these passages about joy?
Ps. 51:12 (footnote)

Prov. 3:5-10

Rom. 5:2-3

Rom. 15:13

I Peter 1:8

Act 8:8

Matt. 2:10 (footnote)

2. What brings God joy?
Ps. 51:16-19

3. What does the Hebrew word "rejoice" mean?
Ps. 2:11 (footnote)

Prophetic Declaration:
Whenever you need encouragement, declare Ps. 119:47. "My passion and delight is in your word, for I love what you say to me."

Chapter 15

"The Search"

1. How far back in time did this search for living water go?
Num. 21:17 RSV

Ps. 87:7 RSV

2. What are we pursuing?
Matt 6:21

3. What do we have to gain in this search? To lose?

4. Where are the living waters found?
John 7:37-39

The Well

1. Detail the different stages the author goes through, beginning with thirst and ending in union with the Living Water Himself.

2. Where do you find yourself on this journey?

3. Do we need to fear going back to the source

What is found there?
Twelfth paragraph

"Engulfed in the Deep"

1. What all is interconnected in this new life of peace with God—
this "peace of the deep?"
Rom. 5:1-2 (footnote)

2. What does this peace enable us to do in times of trouble?
Rom. 5:3-5

Prophetic Proclamation:
Boldly proclaim this last statement of the chapter. As you do that,
you are renewing your mind and speaking forth things which are
not as if they were. Rom. 4:17
You are speaking into your future.

Chapter 16

"Enfolding"

1. How does the Spirit of God feel about us?
James 4:5

2. What are good responses on our part?
James 4:7-8

As God enfolds us in His love, what kind of lifestyle "unfolds"
within us?
Eph. 4: 20-24

The Surrender

1. What price did Jesus pay for our transformation?
John 15:13

When He came in human form, what had He already surrendered?
Phil. 2:6-8

When He first loved us, what condition were we in?

Into what are we being transformed?
Eph. 2:22

2. When Jesus came to Gethsemane, what part of His rights and
His will did He surrender?
Luke 22:42

What are we called to do?
John 13:34 (footnote)

What will be the result?
John 13:35

What will be the benefits of surrendering to God?
Ps. 18:24

Rom. 8:17

3. In summary, what does it mean to be a follower of Jesus?
Luke 9:23-24

4. How are we able to be a follower?
I Peter 2:21 The Message

Prophetic Declaration: This chapter's declaration will make
surrender easier.

Worship Opportunity: The song "I Surrender All" song by Journey
Worship Co.

"Surrender"

1. What are some clues to finishing strong?
Ps. 61:1-4

2. Eph. 1:11, 13

Writing God's Word on your Heart:
Sometimes it is fun to practice in front of a mirror and add
expression and gestures into it.

Chapter 17

"The Fire"

1. As you read the poem ask yourself, "What is the condition of *my* heart?"

2. To whom did the author turn for help?

3. Analyze the steps the Shulamite went through in losing her First Love and then in finding Him again.
Song of Sg. 2:16-3:4

4. What should she have done differently?

What did she do right?

The Burning Fire

1. In this chapter the relationship of friends is highlighted.
Who were the two friends in the next passage?
Ex. 33:11

Friendship speaks of knowing someone. How many times is the
word "know" or "known" used in the first five verses?
Ex. 33:12-23 RSV

In Hebrew thought, the word "yada" (knowing) someone meant
having a personal, intimate relationship with them. Who are two
examples of this?
Gen. 4:1
Gen. 18:10 KJV

2. In our personal relationships with Jesus, what truths encourage
us?
Eph. 1:13-14

Rom. 8:38-39

Does knowing Him on a personal heart level have consequences
for eternity?
Matt. 7:21-23 (footnote f)

Who is our loving Friend who is joined to our hearts and *knows*
us? Prov. 18:24 (footnote d)

Who also had a heart (soul) friendship with God? How quickly did
it develop?
Gen. 5:21-24

3. In paragraph 11, what dampened the writer's intimacy (fire) with her Friend? Give other examples from your own personal experiences.

Worship Opportunity: The song "What a Friend We Have in Jesus" by Joseph Scriven

"The Flaming Fire"

Transformation:
What part does our flesh play in distracting us from intimacy with the King?

How can we counteract those distractions?

Chapter 18

"Renewal"

1. Are you sometimes too hard on yourself? Explain.

Too unrealistic in your expectations?

What is His reaction to your failures?
Ps. 86:15

2. What used to be a part of our old Adam-self?
Col 3:7-9 (footnotes)

Transformation:
If He forgives us, do we have His permission to surrender and release any buried self-hatred?
To forgive ourselves for past mistakes?

Ask the Holy Spirit to open the eyes of your heart and reveal any lies of the enemy that have caused you to hate yourself.

The Washing

1. Transformation is a reoccurring theme in God's Word. What do we learn about that process in the following scriptures?
Eph. 4:10

Ps. 126

Ps. 51 (footnotes)

2. Read I Peter 1:3-4 (footnotes).
Who gives the ultimate restoration?

What are the two results?

3. What is restored here?
Ps. 74:6 (footnote)

4. What transformational journey is described in this chapter?

Prophetic Declarations:
Here are three of God's truths to declare over yourself. They answer the questions:
1. Am I worthy?
II Cor. 5:21—I am the righteousness of God in Christ Jesus.

2. Was I an 'accident' or a 'mistake?'
Ps. 139:13—You formed my innermost being.

3. Am I in charge of remaking myself?
Eph. 2:10—I am God's handiwork.

"The Heart of the Father"

1. What is the heart of the Father toward us?
Luke 15:20

2. What is our part, according to the last paragraph?

Chapter 19

"The Water of Life"

1. In heaven, where does the river of life flow?
Rev. 22:1-2

2. On earth, where does the river of life flow?
Ps. 46:4-5 (footnotes)

3. Read Eph. 4:14-16.
What will flow from Christ?

Where will we be led?

What is our connection with Him?

Worship Opportunity: The song, "I've Got a River of Life" by Jeremy Riddle and Bethel Church

The Waterfall

1. Read again the third sentence and the tenth paragraph.
What can we now experience?
Rom. 5:5

2. What else can cascade over us?
II Peter 1:2

3. As the Spirit cascades over us and pulls us in, what is being restored?
Ps. 51:12 (footnote)

4. Read paragraph eight. What part do we play? What will be the result?

5. Read the first sentence of paragraph ten.
Notice that the Spirit of Jesus is a gentleman. He never forces us, but He always invites us to enter in.

Matters of the Heart:
Set apart some time to calm yourself and sit quietly. Invite the Holy Spirit to join you. Feel free to talk to Him about whatever may be on your heart. Ask Him any questions that come to mind. Listen for His answers. You never have to fear closeness with Him.

Perhaps you may want to write about this interaction in a journal and make this the first of many daily encounters with your Friend.

"Free"

1. Read Gal. 5:16-18 (footnotes).
How are we to yield?

To what?

What will be the result in the natural realm?

What will be the result in the spiritual realm?

Transformation:
Our full freedom is a gift to us, purchased at the cross. Is our realization of this freedom a part of our journey?

Holy Spirit, reveal to us any remaining anchors, tethers or shackles to the old self-life. Release them to Christ, the Forgiver.

Lord, what are some ways we can express our freedom?

Chapter 20

"The Key to Being"

1. Do I trust Him enough to allow myself to be drawn into His Presence?

2. Am I moving in the direction of trust?

3. If not, what can I do about it?

Are there any roadblocks I can move out of the way?

The Union

1. Refer to the third paragraph of this chapter.
What more does scripture have to say about the fullness of God?
Ps. 86:5

Eph. 3:19

Col. 1:19 (footnote)

Col. 2:9-10

2. Col. 3:3-4 Continue to declare this aloud over yourself. The more your ears hear it, the more the truth becomes a reality within you.

Gal. 2:20 Here Paul expands on the same truth we have in Col. 3:3-4. What more does he add?

Song of Sg. 8:14 The last sentence reechoes the same triumphant truth!

3. Why can we now live for God?
Gal. 2:19

Col. 2:11-14 (v. 14 footnotes)

Prophetic Declaration:
What an uplifting statement to inspire us to move back into life!

"Break Out"

1. Matters of the Heart:
As we journey through life, it is easy to create dark, hard shells of self-protection.
What heart hurts have brought darkness inside of you?

In what areas has your heart become hard?

2. What steps can you take to break out of darkness and into freedom?
I John 1: 6-9 (footnote e-f)

Writing His Word on your Heart:
Putting Eph. 3:14-20 in your own words will help you grasp the truth of it.

Chapter 21

"When"

1. What are God's promises to us when we go through hard times?
Ps. 23:4

Is. 43:1-4

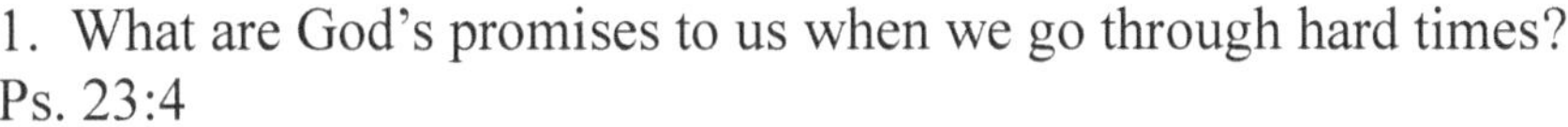

Is. 58:8, 60:1

2. How do we know He identifies with us in every situation?
Heb. 4:14-16

3. What encouragement do we have to keep going on?
Is. 43:18-19

The Knock

1. What is the secret to overcoming all things?
Phil. 4:12-13

Eph. 3:20

Is. 41:13

Col. 3:2

2. Review Col. 3:4.
How, when or where has Jesus revealed Himself to you as He really is?

3. How did it change your life?

Worship Opportunity: The song, "Turn Your Eyes Upon Jesus" by Hillsong Worship.

Prophetic Declaration:
I realize that in Christ I am the conqueror—not fear!

"Rest"

1. What happens when we enter God's rest?
Heb. 4:10 AMPC

2. What is the resting place?
Eph. 3:17

3. How vast is it?
Eph. 3:18-19

4. What will happen when we come to Jesus?
Matt. 11: 28-30 AMPC

5. What is the invitation?
I Peter 5:7

Transformation:
Are fear, grief, trials or hope deferred factors playing into the lack
of rest in my heart?

Can I identify any other factors?

What changes can I make in my life to bring my heart into rest?

Chapter 22

"Swept"

1. Review I Cor. 6:17.

2. What part do we play in the mingling process?
II Cor. 13:11b

Ps. 119:81

Ps. 119:147b

3. Is it a part of Jesus' nature to want to mingle with us?
Matt. 1:23 (footnote)

The Living Word

1. Take a fresh look at the second paragraph of this chapter.

2. Dew is symbolic of what?
Prov. 19:12 KJV

3. Ex. 16:14-15 NIV

4. How much dew was on the grass?

5. How does God go ahead of us to prepare the way?
Is. 45:2-12

Is. 43:16-20

I Cor. 2:9 NIV

Eph. 2:10 NIV

6. In what ways are we to prepare?
I Peter 1:13

I Peter 3:15

Matt. 24:44

II Tim. 4:2 NIV

We can also prepare with this chapter's prophetic declaration.
Is it beginning to seem real to us?

"Your Fire"

1. Where does the fire originate?
Deut. 4:24
Ez.1:4
Rev.1:14
Ps. 18:12-14
Mal. 3:2
Act 2:3

Writing His Word on your Heart:
Write a letter to Jesus. Share with Him the words you've written on
your heart. Let Him know how grateful you are for Him and His
love.
Let His fire ignite your own heart!

Chapter 23

"The Grand Masterpiece"

1. What role does The Grand Overseer play in our lives?
I Thess. 5:24

Phil. 1:6

The Father

1. What kind of Father do we have?
Eph. 3:15

Eph. 4:16

What is the one word both above passages have in common?
Would it be consistent that He would want us to be like Him in this
manner also?

How would you describe a perfect Father?

2. What types of spiritual bread does the Father long to give us?
Ps. 73:26 TPT and NIV

Transformation:
What traps may you have fallen into causing you to push away
your spiritual portion of nutrients? Anger? Disappointment?
Blame?

Who should you be blaming?
John 10:10

In this chapter, what two things did the author do to bring change within herself?

Would this work in your circumstances also?

Worship Opportunity: The song "God is the Strength of my Heart" by Don Moen.

"The Father's Voice"

1. What do we learn about the Father and His relationship with us?
Is. 62:2-4

Zeph. 3:17

Eph. 1:11, 13

John 10:3

James 1:17

2. What comfort do we receive in II Peter 1:10 (footnotes d and e) regarding the Father's claiming us?

3. To what does being a child of the Father entitle us?
II Peter 1:4 (footnote b)

Chapter 24

"The Transformation"

1. What is the ultimate transformation?
II Cor. 5:17 NIV

2. Who does it and how?
Rom. 12:2

3. How did our "Old Creation" express itself?
Eph. 2:3-4

The Encounter

1. What did God use to bring about transformation in this chapter?

2. What do the following verses say about the blood of Jesus?
Eph. 2:13

I Peter 1:19

I John 1:7

Rom. 3:25 (footnote)

Rom. 5:9

Worship Opportunity: The hymn "What Can Wash Away My Sins"
by Robert Lowry

Which childhood songs continue to impact your adult life?

In what ways?

3. Read and meditate on Ps. 32.
In verse 1 (footnote) what is the Hebrew word for forgiven?

Transformation:
Is there anything more for which you need to be forgiven?
If so, bring it to the Lord now.

Is there anything for which you need to forgive yourself?

Take time to do that. You will be amazed at how much better you
will feel after you have released yourself from guilt!

4. What do the following verses say about the awe of God?
Acts 5:11

Ps. 4:4

Ps. 33:8

Mal. 2:5

Ps, 119:161

Ps. 119:120

As a culture, have we lost our awe of God? Why?

"Fire"

1. What was the effect of the fire on these three men?
Dan. 3:19-28

2. What is God's promise to us when we are in the fire?
Is. 43:2

3. What "fire" have you passed through?

What was the outcome?

Chapter 25

"The Grand Adventure"

1. In the following scriptures, who do we have as role models for leaving the past behind?
Did any of these know how the future would "be spread?"
Was their future reward worth what they gave up?
Heb. 11:8

Heb. 11:24-26

Gen. 24:58-60

Gen. 37:28; Gen. 41:51-52

Josh. 2:8-13; Matt. 1:5

Ruth 1:15-17; Matt. 1:5-6

Matters of the Heart;
In what areas have you left the past behind?

What was the result?

The Narrow Place

1. The character trait of humility is highlighted in this chapter.
Who modeled that for us so perfectly?
Matt. 11:28-30
Give examples.

2. In what specific ways have you seen other people doing that?

3. Ask the Holy Spirit how you can practice humility this week.

Matters of the Heart:
What have been some of your narrow places—times of challenge
or testing?

What "baggage" needed to be left behind?

"Victory"

1. Under what banner do we serve?
Song of Sg. 2:4 (footnote)

Worship Opportunity: The song "His Banner Over Me Is Love,"
sung by The Acapella Co.

2. How does this poem fit the days in which we are now living?

3. What good advice is given?

4. In the verses below, who brings the victory?
In what different areas?
II Sam. 23:10-12

Ps. 98:1

I Cor. 15:57

Is. 25:8 TPT and KJV

78

Chapter 26

"Journey of the Will"

1. What part does grace play in our choosing to surrender?
Rom. 6:16a

2. How is grace described?
Rom. 5:15b

Rom 5:16a

Rom. 5:17

Rom. 5:20 (footnote)

The Will

1. Review the chapter and then read Ps. 32:1-7.
When we refuse to yield our wills to God's, is that considered
rebellion? (verse 1)
Can there be, at times, a correlation between the health of our
hearts (mind, will and emotions) and the health of our bodies?
Give examples.

2. What part of the body is symbolic of our will and conscience?
Prov. 3:3 (footnote)

3. How surrendered was the will of Jesus?
John 5:30 AMPC

4. What advice does James give us?
James 4:7,10

5. Try to read Rom. 6:12-23 often this week.
Ask the Holy Spirit to shine His light and give you understanding.
Keep track here of the truths He is revealing.

"Fix It Daddy"

1. Throughout our lives, who is the Great Fixer?
Ps. 3:4

Ps. 61:2

As seen in stanza 3, what is the Father's goal?

According to the psalmist, what all is included in being whole?
Ps. 61:3-4

Chapter 27

"*I AM*"

1. What more do we find out about I AM?
Acts 17:27 (footnotes)

2. What more do we learn about His breath ("Ruach"
in Hebrew)?
John 20:22 (footnote)

Gen. 2:7

Ezek. 37:5-10

Rom 8:11

Transformation:
Practice breathing in the breath of God and exhaling what doesn't belong.
Think thoughtfully about it.
Ask the Holy Spirit to open the eyes of your heart, your godly imagination.
Ask Him to show you what He is doing within you during these times.

The Songs in the Night

1. What is the setting for this time of birthing?
Song of Sg. 8:5

2. Who is the apple tree?
Song of Sg. 2:3
Note: The Bride was already in the shadow of the Bridegroom's
love, but now she is awakened to the fullness of His love for her. It
is a sacred time.
3. What precedent do we have for songs in scripture?
Job 35:10

I Kings 4:32

Col. 3:16

Song of Sg. 1:1

4. Reading the chapter:
As you read it bit by bit, squeeze your eyes shut and see the scenes
played out on the screen of your heart. Begin with the first three
paragraphs.

5. Paragraph four:
Because we are made in His exact likeness, He recognizes the
beauty of His own image resonating in us—like a harmonic chord
on a piano. (His senses are attuned to what He recognizes as
Himself in us.)
Which senses are employed in this paragraph, the next and
paragraph nine?

6. Paragraph five:
We see ourselves represented as doves in these passages.
Song of Sg. 2:14; 1:15; 5:2b; 6:9

Keeping that viewpoint in mind, see yourself in this paragraph.
What is the significance of soaring?
Gal. 5:18 (footnote)

"The Enveloping"

1. Who is the mist, dew, a picture of?
Prov. 3:20

2. What is the Holy Spirit's character?
Gal. 5:22-23

Why do we never need to be afraid of Him?

Chapter 28

"Song of Songs"

1. What two things need to happen before you can dance and soar
in rhythm with His soul?

Where must this take place?

In review, the soul includes what three parts?
Chapter 6

2. This dance is pulsating with what?
I Peter 4:8

3. When you think of your life as a dance instead of a journey,
describe the immediate attitude change that takes place.

Prophetic Declaration:
Look in a mirror and declare this chapter's declaration over
yourself. Continue to speak it forth until your mind, will and
emotions are all in agreement.

Transformation:
Now you can allow yourself to dance and soar with the Dancer of
the Stars. Let it transform you forever.

The High Places

1. Note the invitation at the start of the chapter. It was also in Chapter 14 and Chapter 27.
What is the Lord's advice to us in Ps. 32:8-9.

Matters of the Heart:
What have been your past reactions upon hearing that same invitation?

Describe how your trust in Him has grown since then.

2. Reference paragraph eight.
What was it that set Hezikiah apart from all the other kings of Judah?
II Kings 18:5 AMPC

3. What will be the natural outcome of your trust?
Deut. 31:7-8

"The Hidden Realm"

1. Where is the heavenly realm (the realm of love)?
Heb. 11:16
Eph. 1:3, 20
Col. 3:1

2. Which realm is mentioned in the following verses?
John 3:6

Col. 3:2b

3. Where is the realm in between?
Refer to the ninth paragraph of the chapter and to
Rev. 3:20; Eph. 3:17; John 15:7; John 7:14 KJV.

When we open the doors of our hearts to Jesus, He comes in to
abide and feast with us and we with Him. Our life union with the
Vine creates the hidden place, the realm in between. This is where
the Source of Life resides within us. This is from where the spring
of life bubbles up and then flows as rivers of living water from our
bellies.

Chapter 29

"The World Is Bright With Love"

Matters of the Heart:
Do you remember the first time you fell in love?
Have you longed again for those feelings of wonder, expectation and exhilaration?
As the Bride of Christ, you can allow your heart to be stirred by love once more—the love of the Bridegroom. You will find His heart longing for the same thing.
You *are* worthy, in Him, to love again and to be loved.
Let the world be bright with love!

The Makeover

1. Review paragraphs two and three.
In what ways does the Lord know more about us than we do?
Ps. 139:3-5

Jer. 33:3

2. What heart wounds were healed in this chapter?

3. Does God specialize in divine makeovers? Give examples.
Gen. 17:5-8

Gen. 17:15-16

Gen. 32:24-28

Eph. 2:10

Is. 62:2-5

Eph. 1:8-11

Rom. 8:28-30

I Cor. 15:51-55

4. What do we learn about the final makeover/name change?
Rev. 2 :17 (footnote a)

Rev. 3:12-13

Matters of the Heart:
Think back to a divine makeover you have experienced, either big
or small. Did you need to allow it or cooperate with it? Feel free to
share.

"The Invitation"

1. How well does He know you?
Ps. 139:13-16

Jer. 33:3

Notice the wording of the second to last line.
What more does that tell us?

2. What is your gut reaction to knowing He really does "read my mail?"

3. What does your reaction tell you about your relationship with Him?

4. Are you willing to step out in faith and accept His invitation? (If so, you will never be sorry. Remember, He is a gentleman.)

Chapter 30

"The Living Source"

1. Who is the Source?
Eph. 1:22

I Cor. 1:5-6

Eph. 1:17

Eph. 3:17

What aspect of Christ becomes our very source and root?

Are God and His love separable?
I John 4:16

The Way Of Fruitfulness

1. Where does fruitfulness begin?
I Cor. 15:58

2. Who is our true righteousness?
Col. 1:10

3. How is fruitfulness accomplished? In our own self-effort and strength?
Phil. 3:3b

4. What empowers us?
John 15:10

5. Which virtues will help us be fruitful?
II Peter 1:5-8

6. What do I crave? (Whatever I crave, I will pursue.)
Matt. 5:6

7. What are we not to crave?
I Tim. 6:9-10

Why not?

Matters of the Heart:
Have my cravings brought forth good or bad fruit?

Will that fruit endure?
John 15:16

What is Your plan for me, Lord, as I proceed?

Prophetic Declaration:
"The Holy Spirit once more infuses me with strength, and I know
He will be my help in any situation."

"Finish Strong"

1. Ponder Job 23:10-12.
Write the words here.

2. Are there any mid-course corrections you need to make?

If so, ask the Holy Spirit to help you develop an action plan.

Writing His Word on your Heart:
Let's finish strong as we near the end of our study.

Chapter 31

"Eternity"

1. Our Father is called El Olam, God Eternal. He is God over eternity. That is where our ultimate transformation will take place.

2. Although we were originally created for eternity, will we ever understand the depths of the Creator?
Ecc. 3:11

3. To Ponder: In what ways does the light of God continue to hone (sharpen and perfect) us?

4. What is our purpose?
Is. 43:21 MSG

The Father's Love

1. In Ephesians, the heart of the Father shines through.
The word Father or father is mentioned sixteen times in the six chapters.
2. What do we learn about the Father and ourselves in these verses?
Eph. 1:2b

Eph. 1:3-6

Eph. 4:5-6

Eph. 3:14

3. Recite Eph 3:14-20.

4. What is our response to God's extravagant love?
Eph. 3:21

Eph. 5:20-21

Worship Opportunity: The song, "Children of the Heavenly
Father." It was written by a Swedish woman, Lina Sandell Berg,
who is commonly called the Fanny Crosby of Sweden.

Matters of the Heart:
1. Read the first sentence of the last paragraph.
Notice that as we learn to trust our Father, His love radiates out of
our healed hearts.
What brought about that trust?
Refer to the italicized paragraph.

In what ways have you sensed your trust in the Father growing
throughout this journey?

Trust is the forerunner of intimacy. As you allow Him to dismantle the walls between you, brick by brick, your heart will be healed by His touch, and your future will open before you.

"Home"

An Invitation:
In Luke 15:18 KJV the Prodigal said, "I will arise and go to my father." If you have never been able to say and do that with an earthly father, the door is now open for you to do so with your heavenly Father. Your heart can go home. He is waiting.

1. What help can you ask for on your earthly way home?
Ps. 25:4-7

2. While on this journey, in what practical ways have you, by grace, been able to serve others?
I Peter 4:10

3. What will your homecoming be like?
II Peter 1:11

4. Does your Father intend for this rest to be available to you all the time, even on this earth?
Heb. 4:1-11

95

How is that possible?

Chapter 32

"The Holy Abode"

1. What longing in Chapter 1 is now becoming a reality?

How far back in time does this longing go?
Heb. 11:13-16 NIV

2. Who guides us to our holy abode?
Ex. 15:13 RSV

How does He do it?

3. Who are we to be?
Eph. 5:1

Who is it we are called to imitate?
Eph. 5:2

What pleased God?

What else pleased God?
Heb. 11:4 (footnote o)

The Mighty Flame

1. Refer to paragraph five.
What are the benefits of being a prisoner of love (hope)?
Zech. 9:12; Jer. 16:19

Eph. 5:27 (footnote f)

2. Refer to paragraph seven.
What all is involved in this matter of choosing? Explain it below.
Rom. 6:15-23

3. Give examples of how the relationships of Christian wives and
husbands are parallel to that of the heavenly bride and bridegroom.
Eph. 5:23-33

Transformation:
1. How have the depths of your encounters with the King
increased since the beginning of this journey?

2. Have you allowed yourself to be drawn more and more into His
presence? In what ways?

3. In what areas are you trusting the King now more than before?

4. The heavenly Bridegroom is our divine example of what true love looks like and how it should be expressed. He is Love Incarnate, giving His life for you. Can you now, as His Bride, drop all hesitation and begin to return His love?
He will meet you right where you are. Continue to practice often with Him.

Prophetic Declaration:
"It is well with my soul."
How fitting as we near the end of this journey.

"The Bridegroom"

1. On the first line it says, "You are mine." What new insights are given here regarding these words?
II Peter 1:10 (footnote e)

2. How does this scripture make the concept of bride and bridegroom more real?
I Thess. 4:17 (footnote k)

Writing His Word on your Heart:
Have your memorized verses now taken on a new depth of
meaning? In what ways?

Chapter 33

"The Path"

1. What is the difference between this path and the "interstate of life" in Chapter 1, paragraph three?

What substantial "dust" has the author shaken off her shoes on this journey?

What "dust" of the enemy do you sometimes have to shake off?
Luke 9:5 (footnote)
Matt. 10:14 (footnote)

2. Where has the choice of the traveler in Chapter 1, paragraph four led?

3. Who has assisted her along the way, starting in Chapter 1 and continuing throughout the entire journey? How?
John 14:16-17 (footnotes)

Matters of the Heart:
Looking back, when or how have you recognized the Holy Spirit assisting you along your pathway of life?

Is your answer now different than it was in Chapter 1?

The Purity of Innocence

1. What insights are added here about your journey?
Ps. 139:1-5

Prov. 20:24

2. What are we to wait for?
Ps. 5:3

3. In Gen. 22:5-6 we have the Bible's first mention of the Hebrew word "worship." In the Old Testament, worship always involved sacrifice and fire in the presence of God. (When you are able, read all of Gen. 22 in the Passion Translation.)
What are other examples of sacrifice and fire in worship?

Lev 9:24

I Kings 18:38

II Chron. 7:1

Who is the sacrifice and who is the fire in the following verse?
Song of Sg. 8:6 (footnote)

In the Aramaic, the word "fire" can also be translated as what?
Heb. 12:29 (footnote)

4. Reread the eighth paragraph from the end. "I willingly position myself on the altar."
This is the willing outward sacrifice. Where did we see the inner sacrifice and what was it?
Read Chapter 22, the last paragraph of "The Living Word."

What part does love play in the sacrifice of self?
Matt. 22:37 (footnote g)

5. What is happening in the fifth paragraph from the end?
Ps.17:3

6. How does the Bride now see herself?
Song of Sg. 8:10

How does the Bridegroom-King see her?
Song of Sg. 8:10b

Song of Sg. 4:1b

What is her new purpose in this world?

Song of Sg. 8:10

How do they now see their future together?
Song of Sg. 8:14

"Expansion"

1. Read I Cor. 2:19 and reflect upon the wonders lying ahead. Our human intellect cannot begin to grasp the enormity of Who this King of Love is (Ps. 48:14) and His ever-expanding kingdom of light.
What awaits us is beyond comprehension. To Him be glory forever and ever!
Worship Opportunity: "The Hallelujah Chorus" from Handel's Messiah, sung by the Royal Choral Society

"The Mystery"

1. Go back and review "The Mystery" study for this poem at the end of Chapter 1.
Have you found out Who He really is and who you really are? Give examples.

Transformation Summary:
What have been your personal transformations on this journey?

Do you see more and more hints of His essence in you and at work in your daily life? Give examples.

In what ways have you found yourself becoming more like Him?

2. The beauty of our earthly journey is the "mirror effect."
Read II Cor. 3:18.
When He looks at us, He sees His image reflected. And when we look at ourselves in the mirror, we also see Him peeking through at us.

3. In conclusion, read I Cor. 2:9-16. Here God reveals His heart to us.
Verse 10
Notice the word, "But," connecting verse 9 with the remainder of the passage. What is beyond revelation in the natural realm is accessible by the Spirit.
What is revealed in v. 10?

What does the Spirit of God help us understand and *experience*?
Verse 12

Our words should be coming from where?
Verse 13

What is bypassed?
Verse 14 (footnote)

With the Holy Spirit's help, what are we able to do?
Verse 15

What do we possess and why is that important?
Verse 16 (footnote h)

4. What does it mean to be joined to the Lord?
Read I Cor. 6:17 (footnote).

The mystery revealed is Christ in us, the hope of glory, and we
now one with Him in His glory.
What a Spirit led journey we have experienced together. It is one
that will continue into eternity. All glory and praise to the Author
of all time!

Go to the website https://connievolk.com. Scroll down to the
bottom of the Home Page. The Author of Life is waiting to meet
you in a personal way. Allow yourself to become one with Him.

Reflections of the Author

My prayer for you is that our journey together has been an adventure into the depths of God's heart. It is filled with love for you. He sees you. He knows you. He gave His life for you.

He created the hidden place for us to discover. It is within Him and, at the same time, within us. It is called a deep mystery for good reason. We are always safe there, but it is designed more for our enjoyment and rest than for our understanding. It needs to remain a mystery. If it were totally revealed, what would be left for us to seek?

The excitement of knowing Him is in the revealing of Him. But as soon as we find Him, we realize there is yet more to find! To seek Him is to find Him (Matt. 7:7-8). To know Him is to know who we are, created in His image…the ultimate mystery.

Peace and blessings as you continue your journey with Him.

Connie Volk

For questions or to share with me, go to my website listed above.

Prophetic Declarations